S0-BFE-035

PRAYERS FOR CHRISTIAN SERVICES

Prayers for Christian Services

Carl A. Glover

ABINGDON PRESS New York • Nashville

PRAYERS FOR CHRISTIAN SERVICES

Copyright © MCMLIX by Abingdon Press

Library of Congress Catalog Card Number: 59-5210

SET UP, PRINTED, AND BOUND BY THE
PARTHENON PRESS, AT NASHVILLE,
TENNESSEE, UNITED STATES OF AMERICA

Preface

Prayer is the vital center of worship, and the leader must be in the spirit of prayer if he is to help the congregation into an awareness of the presence of God. Effectiveness in prayer calls for the leader's own spiritual preparation. That is basic. Only as his heart is right can he be better than "sounding brass, or a tinkling cymbal."

The leader in public worship, however, needs more than heart culture in order to ensure the fullest measure of group participation in prayer. He needs mental discipline. He may be sincere and dedicated and yet fail to stir the congregation if his words are stale and commonplace, his sentences formless and discursive, and his spiritual horizons narrow and limited. These failings may be corrected by careful attention to prayer structure and

5

prayer vocabulary. When culture of the heart is reinforced by culture of the mind, the leader should be able to offer prayers whose words are fresh and vigorous, whose sentences are compact, and whose horizons include the various aspects of the kingdom of God.

This book contains a variety of prayers. Starting with the prayer with the choir before the service, the volume includes suggestions for the whole range of prayers for a service of worship down to the prayer which follows the sermon. The book's main emphasis is upon the component parts of the pastoral prayer: thanksgiving, penitence and confession, petition, intercession, and dedication. The pastoral prayer itself may include prayers from some or all of these divisions, as in Chapters XII and XIII. Or, as effectively used in some churches in Scotland, the pastoral prayer may be divided into two sections separated by hymn and scripture. One section would contain prayers limited to penitence and petition, and the other section prayers of thanksgiving, intercession, and dedication.

The chapters headed "The Collect," "Guided Meditation," "Prayer on Specific Scripture," "Certain Days and Occasions," and "Litanies and Responsive Prayers" call for comment.

The moving collect "Almighty God, unto whom all hearts are open, all desires known . . ." is one of the few collects in general use in Free Churches. This collect for cleansing, taken from the Gregorian Sacramentary, has a place at the administration of Holy Communion and is occasionally used as the invocation at regular services of worship. The collect form deserves wider use.

The structure of the collect form gives it strength, beauty, and rhythm. The first collect in Chapter III of this book, prayer number 21, illustrates the usual pattern for this form of prayer: (1) the divine name ("O God"); (2) the relative clause which indicates a specific attribute of God ("who dost reveal thyself to the humble and contrite heart"); (3) the central petition which voices the heart's longing ("grant unto us who seek

7

thy face such a clear vision of thyself"); (4) the secondary petition which carries the central petition further along and names the blessing which will follow ("that we may rest quietly in thy presence"); (5) the ascription ("through Jesus Christ our Lord. Amen").

In addition to its use at Holy Communion or as an invocation, the collect form may serve as an introductory paragraph for the pastoral prayer. It also may be used to petition God's blessing upon the reading of the scripture or as a prayer before or after the sermon.

Guided meditations are growing in favor. A few examples are included in Chapter IX in the hope that they may stimulate the use of this prayer form. A period of guided meditation leads even immature Christians into the spirit of prayer by naming definite prayer objectives, and it encourages congregational participation in the quest for communion with God.

Each of the guided meditations in this book includes four or five sections. Each section follows this pattern: the bidding by the minister; silent prayer; spoken prayer by the minister which is in keeping with the bidding; and "Amen" played by the organist. The "Amen" marks the transition between the end of one section and the beginning of another. The conclusion of all the sections of the guided meditation is indicated by the organist's playing of a hymn prior to the final "Amen." A skilled organist can vary the pitch of the "Amens" yet weave them into a harmonious pattern for the complete meditation. When a guided meditation is to be used, the organist should have a copy in advance so that he may prepare appropriate organ responses.

The specific scriptures on which the prayers of Chapter XI are based are, respectively: a description of the Christian arming for spiritual warfare, a psalm of trust and confidence, and a prayer. The preparation in each instance was identical. The scripture was first analyzed and the sequence of ideas noted, and then the ideas were woven into the form of a modern prayer. A similar plan may be applied to a variety of scriptures. Many of the psalms, already cast in prayer forms, may be reworded so as to give helpful expression to the aspirations of modern man. Familiar passages such as Phil. 4:4-7, Phil. 4:8-9, and I Pet. 1:3-9 are admirable scripture bases for public prayer. The eulogy to love in I Cor. 13:1-7 may readily be adapted to the prayer form. The prayer might begin after this fashion, "O God of love, who hast bidden us love our neighbor as ourselves, grant us grace to fulfill this law of Christ." The address to Deity may be followed by petitions for vision to see that love is greater than personal achievement or even humanitarian service, for love that rises above resentment, and for love that rejoices in goodness, truth, and righteousness. The prayer may come to a fitting close by using verse 7 as a commitment: "Help us in all our doings to show the love that beareth all things, believeth all things, hopeth all things, endureth all things; through Jesus Christ our Lord. Amen."

In Chapter XIII on "Certain Days and Occasions," prayers with a special emphasis have been arranged in such a way that any one section may be used by itself or fitted into a pastoral prayer, or the two sections may readily be woven together into a single prayer for the day.

The litany or responsive prayer is one of the most ancient of prayer forms. The parallel structure of some of the psalms indicates that they were used as responsive prayers either by the cantor and the congregation or by two choirs. The litany is becoming increasingly common in nonliturgical churches both in church services and in small groups. It is more specific than the guided meditation and goes a step further in the matter of congregational participation. In a guided meditation the congregation prays silently, following suggestions made by the leader. In a litany the congregation gives audible, unison responses to specific statements made by the leader, thus participating in the words as well as the spirit of prayer.

The use of a litany or responsive prayer makes it almost imperative that each member of the congregation have a copy of the litany. This drawback may be overcome in small groups by having the leader tell the members of the group the words to be spoken at the end of each section, but even then the spirit of prayer is often lost because of people's uncertainty about their responses. It is hoped that the examples given here will encourage leaders of worship to prepare and use litanies or responsive prayers on specific worship themes.

CARL A. GLOVER

Contents

PRAYERS FOR CHRISTIAN SERVICES

I

Prayer with the Choir Before Service

1

Blessed art thou, O God, and greatly to be praised. Thou hast bidden us rejoice and make melody in our hearts before thee. Inspire us for the coming hour in the sanctuary. Accept the tribute of our heart's devotion. Grant that we may worship thee in spirit and in truth, in love and in gratitude; through Jesus Christ our Saviour. AMEN.

2

O God, our heavenly Father, who hast given us the means of self-expression through our voices; guide us this day in speech and song that we may worthily declare our Christian witness; through Jesus Christ our Lord. AMEN.

3

O Lord, who hast bidden us enter thy house with rejoicing; we thank thee for our share in the hour of worship. Kindle our hearts by thine indwelling presence. Touch our lips that they may sing thy praise. Use our voices to interpret the music of the gospel. And give us wisdom to devote all our talents to the furtherance of thy kingdom; through Jesus Christ. AMEN.

4

God of light and beauty, on this sunlit morning we would not have hearts that are cold or lips that are dumb. Let thy light descend upon us so that doubts and fears and all spiritual darkness may be dispelled. Grant

18

that with joyous hearts and singing lips we may praise thy name; through Jesus Christ our Lord. AMEN.

5

We praise thee, O God, for the power of music to lift us out of our lesser selves. Open our hearts to receive thy message through music. Release us from captivity to meanness and despair and the sins that so easily beset us. Let us enter into the liberty wherewith Christ has made us free. May we worthily proclaim thy glory and joyously offer our sacrifice of praise; through Jesus Christ our Lord. AMEN.

6

We beseech thee, O Lord, to accept the work of our hands, the worship of our hearts, and the songs of our lips. Let us so herald the good tidings of great joy that members of the congregation may be lifted on wings of prayer

19

and praise into thy presence. And grant that they and we may worship thee in the beauty of holiness; through Jesus Christ our Lord. AMEN.

7

Spirit of God, descend upon our hearts that we may glorify thy name in this temple of praise. We would worship thee in the beauty of holiness. Let joy be in our hearts, gratitude upon our lips, and consecration in our souls. We make our dedication in the name of our Redeemer. AMEN.

8

O Lord, who hast bidden us serve thee with gladness and come before thy presence with singing; we beseech thee to draw out the music within us that we may enter into thy gates with thanksgiving and into thy courts with praise. AMEN.

9

We praise thee, O God, that thou hast called us into the service of thy Church. So direct our hearts and minds that we may become instruments of thy purpose. Use us as channels of blessing. Let our voices arouse new hopes, sing great truths, and communicate fresh courage. And may the influence that flows through us serve thy kingdom and magnify thy name; through Jesus Christ our Lord. Amen.

II

Invocation

10

Heavenly Father, who hast bidden us renew our strength by waiting upon thee; we invoke thy blessing as we gather in this place of prayer.

Here we would put aside fretfulness and anxiety and find release from our fears.

Here we would be cleansed from the stain of sin and fortified against the power of temptation.

Here we would calm our spirits in the quiet of the sanctuary and receive the peace that passes all understanding.

Of thy mercy search out our secret prayers,

hear them in love, and answer them as thou seest good; through Jesus Christ our Lord. AMEN.

11

Thou, O Lord, who art the light of the world, the desire of nations, and the shepherd of souls; look upon us with compassion and grant us thy blessing. Enlighten our minds with thy truth, satisfy our hearts with thy love, and feed our souls with thy spirit. Grant that we may know thee as the spring of all comfort, the source of all joy, and the fountain of all blessings; through Jesus Christ our Lord. AMEN.

12

Blessed and eternal God, from whom we come, by whom we are sustained, and to whom we shall return at the close of our pilgrimage; we ask thee to look upon us with favor.

To thee we turn from an unquiet world. We bring our work to be sanctified, our

23

wounds to be healed, our sins to be forgiven, our hopes to be quickened, our better selves to be renewed.

To thee we come as prodigals from the far country. Getting and spending, we have wasted our powers. Content with passing pleasures, we have bartered our heritage for things cheap and common. Forgetting thee, we have lost our heart's true home.

We commend ourselves to thy fatherly goodness. Receive us with compassion. Renew us in faith, hope, and love. Restore unto us the joy of thy salvation. We invoke thy blessing in the name of Jesus Christ our Saviour. AMEN.

13

We thank thee, O Father, for moments of spiritual awareness when the barriers of time have been dissolved and we have caught glimpses of the Eternal. Grant us now in this time of worship grace to enter into the secret place of the Most High. Open our minds to a better understanding of the unseen and eternal. Let us lay hold upon some spiritual treasure. So may this hour be as the gate of heaven to our souls. We pray in the name of our Redeemer. AMEN.

14

God of all grace and truth, who dost speak to man's soul through the still small voice; help us to be quiet before thee that we may be aware of thy presence. Come to our hearts as the spirit of peace, that all storms of passion and murmurs of self-will may be subdued. Enter our lives as the spirit of love, that we may be eager to obey thy commands. Descend upon us as the spirit of truth, that we may gain new insight and understanding, O Lord, our Strength and our Redeemer. AMEN.

15

Eternal God, whose face is hidden from the proud and unbelieving and revealed to those who put their trust in thee; grant unto us a humble and contrite spirit, that we may know thy presence and rejoice in thy goodness.

Help us to be still and know that thou art God, that we may hear thy voice in the silence. Teach us to pray, that our words of prayer and praise may be acceptable in thy sight. Make us responsive to the hallowed associations of this place of prayer, that we may serve thee more worthily. So may we rejoice and find peace and strength in this place of prayer; in Jesus' name. AMEN.

16

Eternal Spirit, whose chosen dwelling is the heart that longs for thee and humbly seeks thy face; we turn to thee in our need for thou art our light and life, our hope and salvation.

We come with our sins to be confessed, our hopes to be renewed, our better purposes to be strengthened, our lives to be reconsecrated.

Descend upon us in gracious power according to our need. Enlighten our minds, strengthen our wills, give peace to our souls, and restore unto us the joy of thy salvation. We offer our prayer in the name of Jesus Christ. AMEN.

17

Merciful Father, whose will it is that all should know thee and in knowing thee should find life eternal; we bow before thee in supplication. Thou hast made us for thyself. We are restless until we rest in thee, lonely until we have fellowship with thee, lost until we find ourselves through thee. Unite us now in the quiet communion of prayer. Renew a right spirit within us that we may worship thee with clean hands and a pure heart. Lead us into a deeper knowledge of thy message to us that we may fulfill thy purpose for our lives. We seek thy blessing in the name of Jesus Christ our Lord. AMEN.

18

O Lord God, who makest thyself known to the waiting heart; grant that in this temple of praise we may feel thy presence and learn thy will. Speak to us through the music and the spoken word. And grant that even in the silence we may hear thy voice.

Speak peace to our souls. Anxious and fretful about many things, we long for peace as the storm-tossed mariner longs for the quiet harbor. Grant unto us the peace that passeth all understanding.

Comfort us with pardon. Burdened by the memory of our transgressions, we long for pardon as the penitent child longs for the kiss of forgiveness. May we know in our hearts that our sin is forgiven and our transgression covered.

Renew confidence within us. Troubled by fears, we long for faith as the hard-pressed warrior longs for assurance. Renew in us the confidence that through thee we shall overcome.

Thou knowest our dreams, our unspoken desires, our secret longings. Hear our cry. And in thine infinite compassion answer our requests according to thy goodness and wisdom; through Jesus Christ our Lord. AMEN.

19

O God our Father, grant unto us who seek thy face such a clear vision of thyself that we may quietly rest in the confidence of thy goodness.

Touch our hearts with reverence and gladness. As we worship in this place of prayer, grant us clearer understanding of thy truth and greater willingness to follow where truth leads. Refresh our souls by a deeper knowledge of him whom to know is life eternal. Inspire us with eagerness to enter into our heritage as thy sons and daughters; through Jesus Christ our Lord. AMEN.

20

Gracious Father, through whose strength we find quietness and confidence; let us sense thy presence in this place of worship.

Here may we touch and handle things unseen. We would enter into the mystery of prayer, hear the still small voice, and refresh our souls at the fountain of living water.

Here we would learn more of life's meaning. We would see afresh the splendor of the eternal quality of life and renew our consecration to the work of thy kingdom. We pray for thy blessing in the all-prevailing name of Jesus Christ our Saviour. AMEN.

III

The Collect

21

For a Vision of God
O God, who dost reveal thyself to the humble and contrite heart; grant unto us who seek thy face such a clear vision of thyself that we may rest quietly in thy presence; through Jesus Christ our Lord. AMEN.

22

For Confidence in God
Merciful Father, who dost bestow upon thy children such gifts as they cannot gain for themselves; grant us the confidence that thou

art loving us in every disaster, lighting our way in every darkness, strengthening us in every weakness, and caring for us in every trouble; through Jesus Christ our Lord. AMEN.

23

For Joy in God

Eternal God, whom to know is to love and whom to love is to find joy; grant us such knowledge of thee that our hearts may be filled with gladness and our faces lighted with joy; through Jesus Christ our Lord. AMEN.

24

For Quietness

Gracious God, who art and wast and art to come; make us sensitive to thy presence that we may be still and know that thou art God; through Jesus Christ our Lord. AMEN.

25

For Salvation

Blessed Saviour, who didst take the form of a servant and, being found in fashion as a man, didst humble thyself unto death, even the death of the cross; deliver us from our sins, we beseech thee, and grant us thy salvation. AMEN.

26

For Power

Eternal Spirit, who dost breathe into man the breath of life and endue him with power from on high; strengthen us with might in the inner man, we pray thee, that our lives may show forth thy praise; through Jesus Christ our Lord. AMEN.

27

For Guidance

Shepherd of the wandering star and faithful guide of all who seek thee, direct us along our

pilgrimage and bring us to him who is the
life, the truth, and the way; through Jesus
Christ our Lord. AMEN.

28

For Concentration

Blessed and eternal God, who hast bidden
us worship thee in spirit and in truth; fortify
us against all distractions that in this hour of
worship we may perfectly love thee and worthily praise thy holy name; through Jesus Christ
our Lord. AMEN.

IV

Thanksgiving

29
The Everlasting Goodness

O Lord, whose mercies are new every morning and fresh every evening; we rejoice in thy goodness.

We thank thee for the mercies of the morning when dawn awakens the earth to beauty and to light, and all creation praises thee. We glorify thee for wider horizons when life's way opens before us in splendor and we see more clearly the path that leads to the Father's house. We praise thee for times of sudden awareness when our hearts are lifted in prayer and we receive the light of thy benediction.

Accept our gratitude for thy lovingkindness and tender mercies. And guide us to respond to thine everlasting goodness by the service of our hands and the devotion of our hearts; through Jesus Christ our Lord. AMEN.

30

The Beauty of the Earth

O Lord, who hast set our lines in pleasant places and given us a goodly heritage; we praise thee for this wondrous world. We thank thee for the beauty of the earth. Thou hast given us the joy of whispering winds and rippling streams, of fragrant flowers and towering hills, of scudding clouds and trees reaching for the sky.

We thank thee for the majesty of the heavens. We rejoice in the sky-born music of a night of stars, the hush of the dawn when the world wakens to the clean freshness of the new day, and the warmth of the sun which causes the earth to bring forth and bud that the sower may have seed and the eater may have

36

bread. For the bounty of creation and the loveliness of nature, we lift our hearts to thee in glad thanksgiving; in Jesus' name. AMEN.

31
Mercies Each New Day

We remember thy constant goodness, O Lord, and rejoice in the love that crowns our days. We thank thee for food, clothing, and shelter, for the protection and comfort of our homes, and for all material benefits. We rejoice in the laughter of children and the contagion of their joy, in friendly folk who enter our lives and gladden us with kindness, and in dear ones whose affection renews our strength and bestows quiet peace. We praise thee for faith and hope and love, for life and light and truth, for courage and aspiration and peace of mind. Thy mercies are more than the stars for multitude. Glory be to thy name, O Lord Most High. AMEN.

32

Life's Venture

O Lord our God, who hast given us the privilege of sharing in life's venture; we lift our hearts to thee in gratitude.

We rejoice in truths to be learned, disciplines to be mastered, battles to be fought, and victories to be won. We rejoice in memories—memories of achievement, of gladness and good fellowship, and memories that cleanse the imagination and satisfy the heart.

We thank thee for homes cheerful with the laughter of children, enriched with the mellowed wisdom of the aged, and joyous with the music of affection. We praise thee for all happy personal relationships. We remember with gratitude our comrades of daily work, companions of leisure hours, friends in high enterprise who renew our hopes and inspire us through good example, and those who interpret the meaning of life and open our eyes to its glory.

Accept our tribute of praise, O Lord, and grant that we may prove our constant grati-

tude by constant fidelity; through Jesus Christ
our Lord. AMEN.

33
Life's Good Things

Thou, O Lord, hast opened thy hand and
satisfied us with good things. We thank
thee for life and health, home and friends,
church and country, the abundance of harvest,
and the goodness and mercy that have been
our constant companions. Thou hast set our
lines in pleasant places, brought us to a good
land, and given us a goodly heritage.

Help us to prove our gratitude by following him who came not to be ministered unto
but to minister. May we look at life through
the eyes of Jesus and show his spirit in our
daily conduct. Quicken our imagination to an
awareness of human need. Teach us to forget
ourselves in service to others. May we share
our abundance with the hungry, open doors
of beauty to the troubled, and extend the
hand of friendship to the lonely. Grant that

we may be wise stewards of the good things thou hast entrusted to us. We offer our prayer in the name of the great Friend of all the children of men, even Jesus Christ our Lord. AMEN.

34

Gratitude for God's Goodness

Thou, O Lord, art the giver of every good and perfect gift. Thou hast called us to the adventure of life, sustained us by thy providence, chastened us by thy discipline, and redeemed us by thy love.

We thank thee for life with its mystery and wonder, its friendships and activities, its splendor and satisfactions. We thank thee for food, raiment, shelter, and all the material benefits of thy providence. We thank thee for burdens which increase our strength, for hindrances that turn our steps away from evil, and for all discipline that brings us closer to thee. We thank thee for the divine light that shone in the face of Jesus, the divine spirit

40

that showed in his teachings, and the divine love that made him obedient unto death, even the death of the cross. Our tribute of praise we offer in the name of our Saviour. AMEN.

35
Christian Citizens

God of all goodness, who dost use thy servants to advance human welfare; we thank thee for all faithful followers of him who went about doing good.

We remember with gratitude those who minister to the sick and handicapped in places of healing. We thank thee for those whose compassion leads them to care for the needy and underprivileged. We rejoice in those who seek to bring about better relations between management and labor. We praise thee for those whose concern leads them to attack ancient wrongs and to serve the common good by promoting racial understanding.

For all thy servants whose devotion stirs our better selves, we lift our hearts in gratitude.

Give us grace to stand by them, to work with them, and to prove that we have passed from death unto life because we love the brethren; for the sake of Jesus Christ our Lord. AMEN.

36

World Brotherhood

Dear Lord and Father of mankind, who hast committed to thy Church the task of proclaiming the good news of the kingdom to every race and nation; we rejoice in the day of dawning brotherhood.

We thank thee for thy servants in every land whose lives, sustained by prayer and worship, are radiant centers of spiritual healing. We praise thee for teachers, missionaries, and all heralds of good tidings who feed men's souls with the Word of life. We give thanks for men and women whose friendship reaches across chasms of resentment and suspicion and promotes good will among men and nations.

Increase the desire for peace in the hearts of all men. Guide the leaders of the nations by thy wisdom. And grant that good government and righteousness may flourish in every land and that brotherhood may be a joyous reality among all races and peoples. We offer our prayer in the name of him who is the Light of the world. AMEN.

37

The Christian Heritage

Blessed and eternal God, from whom we come, by whom we are sustained, and to whom we shall return; we thank thee for the good things bequeathed to us by the journeying generations. Others labored, and we have entered into the profits of their labor. Churches we did not build are centers for our worship and inspiration. Liberties we did not earn are our birthright. Truths we did not discover are a lamp to our feet and a light upon our path.

As we have freely received, so may we freely serve. Make us wise in the arts of stewardship. Grant that we may so live and work that those who come after us shall rejoice that we passed this way; through Jesus Christ our Lord. AMEN.

38

The Local Church

O God, who hast kindled in thy servants the great hope that thy kingdom shall come and thy will be done on earth as it is in heaven; we rejoice in the message and ministry of this church. We thank thee that in this place little children have been dedicated to thee, young people have caught the vision of Christian ideals, mature men and women have received spiritual reinforcement, and the aged have found light at eventide.

Continue to use the fellowship of this church, we pray thee, for the ongoing of thy kingdom. Let thy Spirit dwell in our midst and be our constant inspiration. Make us willing to accept our responsibility to those who come within the range of our influence.

Give us skill in Christian conduct. Show us how to extend sympathy to the troubled, friendship to the lonely, and understanding to the tempted. So may we communicate love and joy and peace for the sake of Jesus Christ our Lord. AMEN.

39

Road Builders

We remember with gratitude, O Lord, thy servants who faithfully build the Christian highway. We thank thee for parents who train children in Christian ways, for educators who direct inquiring minds into paths of truth, and for public leaders who rally the people around the banner of righteousness. We praise thee for missionaries who preach the gospel as the power unto salvation, for church workers whose lives are a constant inspiration, and for all who prepare the way for the Saviour of mankind.

Grant that these thy servants may see the

fruits of their labor and be satisfied. May they have the confidence that thy word cannot fail and that it must accomplish thy purpose. Inspire them with the assurance that every valley shall be exalted, every mountain and hill brought low; that the crooked shall be made straight and the rough places plain; that thy glory shall be revealed. We offer our praise in the name of our Saviour. AMEN.

40

Christ's Interpretation of Life

Infinite Father, who hast set the span of our years within the heart of thine eternity; we praise thee for the Master's interpretation of human life. We thank thee for the message which makes plain the path of duty, for the teaching which reveals sources of power, and for the winged words which tell of life's greatness.

Give us grace to respond to the Master's vision. Open our eyes to the glory of life as it may be lived. May we find meaning in the commonplace, beauty in lowly places, and opportunities in the everyday. Grant us better understanding of the height and depth, length and breadth, and everlasting splendor of the life thou has given us; through Jesus Christ our Lord. AMEN.

41

Christ the Redeemer

O God, who hast redeemed us through the mystery of the cross; we bow before thee in reverent gratitude for the revelation of thy love declared in Jesus Christ. We praise thee that he shared our common life and humbled himself and became obedient unto death, even the death of the cross. We bless thee that he bore our griefs, carried our sorrows, and triumphed over sin and death. We glorify thee that through his perfect and sufficient sacrifice on the cross there is pardon for the penitent, power to overcome for the faithful, and transformed life for all who truly turn to him.

Give us grace to yield ourselves in glad surrender to the Lord Jesus. May we share his spirit of obedience to thy will, his consecration to the welfare of humanity, and his passion that thy kingdom may come and thy will be done on earth as it is in heaven. So may Christ dwell in our hearts and reign there as our divine Redeemer. AMEN.

V

Penitence and Confession

42

Awareness of Failure

Gracious Father, who hast made us for thyself so that our hearts are restless until they rest in thee; we beseech thy favor. Our lives are as an open book to thee, and nothing is hidden from thy sight.

Thou knowest the desires that pass through our minds, stir in our hearts, and tremble upon our lips. Thou knowest our longings to live more nearly as we pray. We would be true and worthy of trust. We would be generous and forget the gift. We would be humble and put aside boasting. We would stand up for our Master and follow his banner.

With penitence we confess our failures. We have left unguarded the doors of our imagination and permitted evil thoughts to wander down dark paths and forbidden ways. We have lacked self-control and permitted our tongues to betray us in anger. We have crept from the battlefield and permitted others to bear the shock of the struggle.

Look upon us in mercy. Forgive us for our failures. Strengthen us in high resolve. Renew a right spirit within us. And help us to love thee with all our heart and strength, soul and mind, and to love our neighbor as ourselves. We offer our prayer in the Saviour's name. AMEN.

43

Turning from the Light

O Lord God, who hast ordained that the Sun of Righteousness shall arise with healing in his wings for them that seek after thee; lighten our darkness, we beseech thee, that every shadowed corner of our lives may be bright with thy presence.

Our joy has been dimmed, for we have disobeyed thy commandments and lost the light of faith. Desolation has fallen upon us, for we have strayed from thy paths and turned from the light of hope. Loneliness has been our lot, for we have companioned with evil and rejected thy love.

May the dayspring from on high visit our waiting hearts. Renew us in faith and hope and love. And restore unto us beauty for ashes, joy for sorrow, and light for darkness; through Jesus Christ our Lord. AMEN.

44

Penitence for Disobedience

O Lord our God, who makest thyself known to the longing heart and humble spirit; we confess our rebellion and turn to thee in penitence.

Thou didst open to us the path of righteousness, and we willfully turned aside to paths of error and darkness. Thou didst grant us the glowing vision of life as it ought to be lived, and we failed to measure up to the standard. Thou didst assure us that as our day so should our strength be, but we doubted thy promise and in the hour of need failed to gather spiritual reserves.

Look upon us in compassion. Pardon us and renew our inner strength. And grant that in the days to come we may rejoice in obedience to thy commandments; for thy name's sake. AMEN.

45

Confession of Unworthiness

Merciful Father, who desirest not the death of the sinner but that all should be delivered from the haunting memories of transgression; look upon us in compassion as we confess our unworthiness.

We have drawn back from serving thy children and turned aside from opportunities to help. We have failed to extend friendship to the discouraged and have allowed watching eyes to grow dim and eager hearts to become sad. We have neglected to bear our brother's burden and suffered him to be bowed down because we have not cared enough.

Forgive us that we hid our talent in the earth, that we neglected our responsibilities, that we left undone the things we ought to have done. And grant that through the renewing power of thy pardon we may find again the new life in Christ that is deep and pure and true. In his name we pray. AMEN.

46

The Stained Record

Most holy Father, who knowest our frame and rememberest that we are dust; have mercy upon us as we open before thee the stained record of our days.

We acknowledge our blunders. We have seen the vision of life's glowing possibilities and with high hopes have resolved to fulfill the dream. But our will has weakened, and our hopes have faded. We confess our failures. We have seen opportunities for service and have meant to fulfill our better purposes. But our good intentions have fallen by the wayside, and we have been false to our better nature.

Still thou dost believe in us, love us, and show us the way of life. Forgive us for our broken purposes. Cleanse our hearts from the stain of evil. Pardon us for the wrong we have done and the good we have left undone. And grant us thy salvation; through Jesus Christ our Lord. AMEN.

47

Sorrow for Shortcomings

O Lord, who searchest the heart and knowest our frailties; with shame we confess our shortcomings. We have seen opportunities for service but evaded responsibility. We have heard the trumpet call but deserted the battlefield. We have known the truth but yielded to the false.

Have mercy upon us for delinquent loyalties, limping progress, deliberate disobedience.

54

Forgive us for broken vows, unfulfilled promises, and shattered ideals. Pardon us for being too busy with trifles to lay hold on things eternal, too dull to hear the songs of Zion, too slow to catch the vision of the Holy Grail.

Strengthen us in the inner man, we pray thee, that we may put away all hurtful things and steadfastly endeavor to do thy will; through Jesus Christ our Lord. AMEN.

48

Regret for Bartered Birthright

Every knee shall bow before thee, O Lord, and every tongue shall confess that thou art God. We approach thy throne as children come to a father who is wise and gracious, tender and compassionate. We believe that thou shalt come to be our Judge. We therefore pray thee, help thy servants as we bow before thee in the name of him who bore the cross for man's salvation.

We are troubled by the memory and burden of our offenses. We have spent our money for that which is not bread and our labor for that which satisfies not. We have bartered our birthright and scorned our heritage for that which yields no profit. And we have turned aside from paths of righteousness.

Mercifully grant us thy pardon. Calm our troubled souls. And let the beauty of thy peace, the peace that the world can neither give nor take away, descend upon our hearts; through Jesus Christ our Redeemer. AMEN.

49

Contrition for Inertia

O God, who hast promised forgiveness of sins to those who are truly penitent; we humbly confess our frequent folly and failure. We have denied the promptings of our hearts and have done those things which we ought not to have done.

We have made good resolutions, but failed to express them in action. We have volunteered to serve those in need, but when opportunity came, we passed by on the other side.

56

We have promised to be always faithful, and instead of standing by our Master, we have warmed ourselves at enemy campfires. For foolish boast and frantic word, thy mercy on thy people, Lord.

Deliver us from apathy. Forgive our indifference. Send tides of power into our waiting souls. Stir the warrior blood in our veins and instill in us the strength of will to match our high purpose. We ask in the name of him who bid us work while it is day, even Jesus Christ our Lord. AMEN.

50

The Good Left Undone

O God, who hast enlightened us and shown us the path wherein we should walk; we have erred and strayed from thy ways like willful children.

We have given our hearts away for the pleasure of the passing hour and neglected things splendid and eternal. We have insisted upon claiming our rights and neglected our responsibilities. We have cultivated wisdom according to the flesh and neglected the wisdom that belongs to our peace.

With shame we confess the harm we have done and the good we have left undone. With contrition we commend ourselves to thy compassion and pray for forgiveness. Humbly we beseech thee to restore unto us the joy of thy salvation; through the merits of Jesus Christ our Redeemer. AMEN.

VI

Petition

51
For the Help of Christ

Thou, O God, hast bidden us find our true life through thy Son, who is the Pioneer of our salvation. Grant us grace to set him at the center of our thinking and to put our trust in him.

When the inner light grows dim in times of sadness, and shadows drift across our minds, may the darkness be dispelled by him who is the Light of the world. When joy refreshes our hearts in times of gladness, may our happiness be increased through fellowship with him who gives the life more abundant. When temptation troubles us in times of moral confusion, may we endure as seeing him who is invisible.

Quicken us to know Christ and the power of his resurrection, that through his help we may walk in newness of life; for thy name's sake. AMEN.

52

For Wider Horizons

O God, guardian of all our yesterdays and hope of all our tomorrows; we beseech thee to open our minds to wider horizons. Liberate us from the narrow views of an outgrown past. Make us willing to learn new truth and eager to serve the present age in the awareness that new occasions teach new duties. So may our mental horizons be enlarged, our practical endeavors be extended, and our Christian service be increased. We ask in the name of him who gives the truth that makes men free, even Jesus Christ our Lord. AMEN.

53

For Joy in Common Days

We need thee every hour, most gracious Father. Give us a singing sense of thy presence as we engage in the daily round and common task. Forbid that we should despise the day of small things. May we be cheerful as we walk in familiar paths. And let us seek to obey thy will whether we actively serve or only stand and wait. So may we be faithful in common days and find joy in common tasks. We ask in the name of the divine Carpenter of Nazareth. AMEN.

54

For Strength to Endure

We pray for thy favor, O Lord, when we leave familiar ways and enter upon days of tension. Make us strong to endure stress and strain. Give us wisdom to hold fast that which is good and courage to stand firm as good soldiers of Jesus Christ. And through all the strange adventures of our times be thou our strength and stay; for thy name's sake. AMEN.

55

For Adventures in Friendship

O thou great Friend of all mankind, we pray for guidance in the arts of friendship. Help us to break through any reserve, to overcome any timidity, and to extend the hand of friendship to those who come within the range of our influence. So may we welcome opportunities for service, share in the happiness of associates, and give practical expression to our sympathy for those in trouble; through Jesus Christ our Lord. AMEN.

56

For Understanding Sympathy

O Thou who appointest to every man his work, we remember before thee our friends and associates and pray that we may look upon them with eyes of appreciation.

Give us understanding sympathy with those whom we meet on life's highway. By the knowledge of our own shortcomings, guide us to deal gently with their faults. By the memory of our own struggles, prepare us to sympathize with them in their difficulties. By the awareness of our own joy, make us responsive to their rejoicing.

Teach us the arts of kindness that we may do unto others as we would they should do unto us; through Jesus Christ our Lord. Amen.

57
For Sensitive Spirits

Make us alert to thy presence, O Lord. Let thy voice speak to us through our worship. May the moments of silence be filled with messages from thee. Teach us to profit by the kindling thought, the fugitive inspiration, the glowing word. Grant that through obedience to thy word we may weave strength and beauty into the tapestry of our lives; through Jesus Christ our Lord. Amen.

58
For Courage

Lord of the hopes of all the years, who hast bidden thy servants wait upon thee and find good courage; grant unto us who seek thy face serene hope and victorious courage.

Give us grace to rise above inner weakness, that we may be fitted to fulfill thy plan for our lives. Make us crusaders for justice, that we may promote human welfare among peoples of every race and class. Fortify us against pessimism, that we may march breast forward in the confident hope that wrong shall pass away and righteousness prevail.

Inspire us with the spirit of the Master as we face the hindrances, handicaps, and petty irritations of the common day. So may we be more than conquerors through him who loved us and gave himself for us. We present our petition in the name of him who was victorious over sin and death, even Jesus Christ our Saviour. AMEN.

59

For Awareness of God

Eternal Father, who in a world of change hast set eternity in our hearts and given us a spirit that answers to thine own; we beseech thee to deepen our awareness of thee.

Quicken our understanding to see thy work in creation. The healing of the sunshine, the music of the rain, the whisper of the wind, are all from thee. Thine is the beauty of the earth and thine the glory of the sky. Thine is the wonder of tree and flower, river and mountain. And all created things are thy handiwork. Glory be to thy name, O Lord Most High.

Help us to know thee through the ministries of human affection. We gratefully recall the unselfishness of parents, the devotion of friends, and the confidence of children. And we remember the patience and understanding of teachers. Teach us to find in these things the reflection of thy love for mankind.

Give us the confidence that thou dost direct the paths of those who acknowledge thee in all their ways. May we remember that we are precious in thy sight, that thou art our guide through the joys and sorrows of the unfolding years, and that thou dost bring thy servants to their desired haven in peace. We offer our

petition in the name of Jesus Christ our
Saviour. AMEN.

60
For Guidance

Eternal Father, who art the true Guide of
all who put their trust in thee; we commend
ourselves to thy gracious keeping. Guide us
when we come to the crossroads of good and
evil. Help us to choose the better part. And
direct our feet into paths of righteousness and
truth, goodness and love.

Give us understanding when we must deal
with life's crises. Deliver us alike from linger-
ing doubt and hasty decision. Inspire us with
calmness and self-control. And so direct our
thinking that we may worthily magnify thy
holy name.

Be our leader as we move into the un-
known future. Whether we meet adversity or
prosperity, grant us the awareness of thy
presence. Preserve us in our going out and
our coming in from this time forth and even

forevermore. We offer our petition in the name of Jesus Christ our Saviour. AMEN.

61

For the Joy of Fulfillment

O Lord, Keeper of the hidden springs of joy and life; we pray thee to look upon us with favor. Open our eyes to the beauty and light of the outer world. Teach us to reap the harvest of a quiet eye and to find joy in simple things and beauty in unexpected places.

Grant us the royalty of inward happiness. May our satisfactions come from quietness and confidence and spiritual understanding. Help us in whatsoever state we are therewith to be content.

Thou hast spread before us a bountiful table. Thou hast unsealed waters from the well of salvation. Thou hast given us songs in the night of sorrow and hast made known to us the ways of life. Give us grace to enter into our heritage as thy children and to find in thee the fulfillment of our lives; for thy name's sake. AMEN.

VII

Intercession

62
For Lives Set to Minor Music

Father of all mercies and God of all compassion, we pray for thy blessing upon those whose lives are set to minor music. We remember the crippled, who face today another day of pain and handicap; invalids, whose pulse of life beats thin; and the handicapped, who feel unequal to life's demands.

We remember before thee the refugees, who are denied home and country; the blind, who are denied the beauty and light of the day; and the bereaved, who are denied the fellowship of dear ones.

Let the angel of thy presence comfort all whose joys this day are limited, whose lives are set to a minor key. Lift upon them the light of thy countenance. Renew them in faith and hope, in courage and understanding. We offer our intercession in the name of Jesus Christ our Redeemer. AMEN.

63

For Those Under Strain

Hear our prayer, O Lord, for the burdened, bewildered, and lonely, and for all who endure stress and strain. Open their hearts to know that thy love is equal to their deepest need. Quicken their minds to receive the strength that matches their heaviest burden. Enlarge their vision to take in the divine light that is shed upon their darkest valley. May they rest quietly in thee in the knowledge of thy goodness. Give them the confidence that thy tenderness is from age to age the same and that thy mercy endures forever; through Jesus Christ our Lord. AMEN.

64

For the Distressed

God of all comfort, we commend to thy compassion those who are distressed in body, mind, or spirit. When they tread weary ways of pain, give to them understanding and patience that they may be preserved from bitterness and given power to endure. When they are perplexed and at a loss to know the right thing to do, open to them fresh channels of hope that they may go forward with rejoicing. When they are discouraged and stricken in spirit, lead them to the living fountains of water that their souls may be restored.

Let thy blessing rest upon all sufferers. May they see the clearing sky, feel confidence in thy goodness, and be strengthened with the faith that gives the victory. We offer our intercession in the name of him who conquered pain and death, even Jesus Christ. AMEN.

65

For the Sick and Suffering

O God, whose ears are ever open to the cry of thy children; hear our prayer for those who are turned aside from the main stream of activity. Comfort the sick and suffering with the assurance of thy presence. Give them the firm faith that they are precious in thy sight. May they know that thy mercy never fails, that thy love is always with them, and that thy goodness and mercy shall be their constant companions. So may they be strengthened in patience, confidence, and peace. We ask in the name of the great Physician, even Jesus Christ our Lord. AMEN.

66

For the Children

O Lord our God, in the name of him who bid the children come unto him, we ask thy blessing upon the boys and girls. Guard them from harm. Supply them with good things. And grant that the unfolding years may bring them strength and beauty of character; for the sake of Jesus Christ our Lord. AMEN.

67

For Students

To thy gracious favor, O Father, we commend the young people attending school and college. Direct them in all their ways. Prosper them in their quest for learning and in their search for life's high values. As they increase in knowledge, may they grow also in wisdom. And grant that they may learn to do justly, love mercy, and walk humbly with thee. AMEN.

68

For Families and Friends

O God, who hast knit us together in the bundle of life; we remember before thee those who are bound to us by ties of dear affection. Let thy favor rest upon members of our families and the friends whose names are upon our hearts. Be thou their light in darkness, their comrade in loneliness, their hope in weariness. Fortify them in temptation, support them in weakness, and be their joy at every step along life's way. May they ever serve thee and love thee, honor thee and glorify thee; through Jesus Christ our Lord. AMEN.

69

For Comrades on Life's Highway

O Lord, who hast given us travel companions along life's highway; we pray that we may be used to convey some special blessing to them.

We remember before thee those who have the light of the dawn upon their faces and songs of joy upon their lips. May we add to their gladness by rejoicing with them. Our hearts go out in sympathy to those who move with painful steps and slow. Show us how to comfort them with acts of kindness and words of healing. We call to mind the good soldiers of Jesus Christ who endure hardness in the cause of truth and justice and righteousness. May we encourage them with words of cheer and support them by standing with them in the fight. These things we ask in the name of him who is the pioneer and perfecter of our faith, even Jesus Christ. AMEN.

70

For the Armed Forces

We beseech thy blessing, O Lord, upon members of the armed forces, especially those who serve in places of peril. Inspire them with prudence and fortitude. Whether they serve on land, in the air, on the seas, or under the seas, may they know that thou art acquainted with them in all their ways. And give them the confidence that the eternal God is their strength, their refuge, and their everlasting home. We offer our prayer in the name of the Captain of our salvation, even Jesus Christ our Lord. AMEN.

71

For the Nation

O Lord, let thy favor rest upon our country. We thank thee for the spirit of those who established the foundations of this nation in righteousness. We praise thee for the courage of those who have defended the country by land and sea and air that liberty might not perish from the earth. And we rejoice in the devotion of all citizens who have served in common ways of every day and in stirring times of national emergency. Continue thy blessings, we pray thee. Guide and uphold our President and those to whom the people have entrusted powers of government. Increase in our citizens the desire to promote mercy and justice, peace and freedom, good will and brotherhood. And grant that our nation may become increasingly a blessing to mankind. We offer our prayer in the name of the Prince of Peace. AMEN.

72

For the United Nations

Infinite Father, who has taught us that we are members one of another; look in blessing, we pray thee, upon the United Nations and all agencies that work for righteousness and peace.

We thank thee for dedicated persons who out of bitter memories of war have been captured by the vision of a peaceful world. Let thy Spirit so move among men that leaders in every nation shall use peaceful means in the effort to establish justice, maintain order, and settle disputes.

May the peoples of the earth learn that peace depends upon good will, that true prosperity must be founded upon righteousness, and that except the Lord build the house they labor in vain that build it. We offer our prayer in the name of the Prince of Peace. AMEN.

73

For Missionaries

O Thou who hast made of one blood all the nations of the earth, we commend to thy goodness all messengers of the gospel. Especially do we pray for the missionaries known and loved by us who make thy ways known to people of strange customs and alien speech. Guide them in perplexity. Support them in weakness. Encourage them in adversity. Preserve them by day and by night. And support them continually with the joy of knowing that they serve thy will. We offer our intercession in the name of the Good Shepherd who died and rose again that there might be one flock and one Shepherd. AMEN.

74

For Those Who Long for Righteousness

Almighty God, the source of all truth and righteousness and peace; hear us in our supplications for those who long for the good life.

Let thy Spirit guide those who, halting between two opinions, hesitate in the valley of decision. Help them to know that the Master's yoke is easy and his burden is light. Quicken them to make the supreme choice. Open their eyes to see and their hearts to accept thy Son as the life, the truth, and the way.

Grant thy favor upon those who seek after righteousness. Teach them to use the dead past as steppingstones to a better future. Lead them to devote their powers to the service of humanity. And inspire them to find in thee their strength and their salvation.

Bestow thy blessing upon those who long for the beauty of thy peace. Comfort them in trouble. Deliver them in temptation. Lift upon them the light of thy countenance. And garrison their hearts with the peace that the world can neither give nor take away; through Jesus Christ our Lord. AMEN.

VIII

Dedication

75
The Arts of Service

O God, who hast given us the privilege of serving thee; grant us grace to follow more perfectly the way of Jesus Christ. Increase our skill in the arts of service. Show us how to impart confidence to those in trouble, faith to those who doubt, hope to those who despair, and courage to those who stumble. Use us as instruments of thy peace. Teach us to be worthy ambassadors of the great Friend of all mankind, and send us forth as heralds of good will. We offer our dedication in Christ's name. AMEN.

76

The Divine Companion

God of our years, whose presence is everywhere and whose goodness never fails; grant us such awareness of thy nearness that we may know thee as our constant Companion and Counselor.

Keep us faithful in the day of monotonous tasks that we may be serene and untroubled. Make us equal to heavy burdens and extended demands, that our strength may be equal to our tasks.

Give us an understanding heart that we may accept good health and vigor and prosperity as the gifts of thy love. Fortify us in the hour of testing that we may accept disappointment or defeat or trouble as discipline for the soul.

Inform our minds with divine truth that we may pattern our lives after the perfect example of the Lord Jesus. And grant that in all things we may endure as seeing him who is invisible. We make our dedication in the name of our Redeemer. AMEN.

77

Watchers for the Dawn

Thou, O Lord, who dost appoint to every man his work, hast commissioned us to be watchmen for the dawn. To thee we dedicate our powers.

Give us grace to be faithful to our task as we stand on the battlements of time. Make us alert to see the dawn's early light, wise to interpret every sign of promise, and eager to share the good tidings of faith and hope. Keep us true to our mission as heralds of the eternal Sun of Righteousness through whom we find healing and redemption; for thy name's sake. AMEN.

78

Through the Eyes of Jesus

O God, who hast taught us to think not only of ourselves but also of our neighbors; awaken our sympathies that we may look at mankind through the eyes of Jesus. May we see that little children need affection, young

81

people need inspiration, the lonely and destitute need friendship, and the troubled need peace.

Make us wise in the attempt to minister to human need. As we look at mankind through the eyes of Jesus, may we also serve mankind with the Master's spirit of compassion. We offer our consecration in the name of the Son of man who came not to be ministered unto but to minister and to give his life a ransom for many. AMEN.

79

More Than Conquerors

Gracious Father, whose will is our salvation and whose way is our peace; grant us patience and courage and faith that we may be more than conquerors through him who loved us and gave himself for us.

Keep us steady in the simple living of our days. With patience may we discipline our wills, cultivate our minds, and harness our powers. So may we be worthy instruments of thy purpose as we take up the common activities of every day.

Make us equal to life's crises. Let us not shrink from our responsibilities. Fortify us with valor to meet handicap, frustration, and conflict. May we conduct ourselves on life's field of honor as good soldiers of Jesus Christ.

Give us faith in life's greatness as we march into the future. Save us from impatience in the day of small things and from fear in times of peril. Make us strong to endure. Help us to march breast forward in hope and courage, faith and confidence. We make our dedication in the name of Jesus Christ, the Captain of our salvation. Amen.

80

The Example of Christ

O Lord God, who hast called us through the teachings of thy Son to work while it is day; help us to shape our lives according to his example.

As Jesus unsealed sources of joy in those he met by the seashore and in the city streets and country lanes of Galilee, so may we evoke gladness in those who come within the range of our influence. As our Master showed friendship to the weak and tempted, the discouraged and dispossessed, so may we extend a helping hand to those in need. As the Saviour dedicated himself and all his powers to the doing of thy will, so may we surrender ourselves to thee in Christian obedience.

Thou knowest, O Father, the duties that await us, the motives that move us, and the aspirations that allure us. Strengthen us that we may worthily serve beneath the banner of the Prince of Peace. And bring us, O King Eternal, into closer fellowship with him who is the life, the truth, and the way. AMEN.

81

Commitment

Keeper of our years and Lord of our lives, we commit ourselves to thee in the confidence

84

that in everything thou dost work for good
with them that love thee.

Sustain us in the daily round and common
task that we may fulfill familiar routine with
cheerfulness. Keep us alert and sensitive when
we engage in fresh ventures that in all our
work begun and continued in thee we may
glorify thy name.

Help us to see more deeply into the meaning of life that we may receive more light and
truth and be more responsive to the teachings
of thy word.

Strengthen us in the hour of temptation
that we may be victorious over evil. And bring
us at last to our goal in peace that we may
have a safe lodging and a holy rest; through
Jesus Christ our Lord. AMEN.

IX

Guided Meditation

82

Scripture: Num. 6:22-27 (Aaronic Blessing)

Organist (softly) : One verse of "Prayer Is the Soul's Sincere Desire"

Minister: In these quiet moments of meditation each person silently offers his own prayers. Let us pray:

Let us remember the special blessings we have received from the hand of God and offer our tribute of thanksgiving.

Minister and Congregation: Silent prayer

Minister: For the love which crowns our days, O Lord, we give thee thanks and praise thy name.

Organist: Amen

Minister: Let us confess our sins and pray for God's forgiveness.

Minister and Congregation: Silent prayer

Minister: Gracious art thou, O Lord, and full of compassion. Blot out our transgressions and cleanse us from sin.

Organist: Amen

Minister: Let us offer our petitions for those in loneliness and trouble and pray that they may have courage and peace of mind.

Minister and Congregation: Silent prayer

Minister: Hear our prayers, O Lord, for those who have a place in our sympathies and grant unto them the joy of thy salvation.

Organist: Amen

Minister: Let us bring to God the special things we desire to have fulfilled in our own lives and in the lives of those dear to us, and pray that he may answer our prayers according to his wisdom and love.

Minister and Congregation: Silent prayer

Minister: To thee, O Lord, shall be all honor and glory now and evermore.

We offer our petitions in the name of Christ the Redeemer.

Organist: One verse of a hymn with Amen

83

Scripture: Hab. 3:2, 17-18

Organist (softly): One verse of "O Jesus, Thou Art Standing"

Minister: As we quietly wait upon God, each person makes his own silent prayer. Let us pray:

Let us pray for ourselves that we may put aside anxiety, trouble, and all hurtful things, and find the peace of God which the world can neither give nor take away.

Minister and Congregation: Silent prayer

Minister: Lift us above fretfulness and care, O Lord, and grant that our ordered lives may reflect the beauty of thy peace.

Organist: Amen

Minister: Let us pray for our friends that according to the wisdom and love of God their hopes may be realized and their desires fulfilled.

Minister and Congregation: Silent prayer

Minister: Hold our friends in thy gracious keeping, O Lord; preserve them in their goings out and their comings in from this time forth and forever.

Organist: Amen

Minister: Let us pray for our church that it may worthily worship God and increasingly serve the needs of this generation.

Minister and Congregation: Silent prayer

Minister: Grant thy blessing, O Lord, upon thy Church that she may successfully meet the challenge of these times.

Organist: Amen

Minister: Let us pray for our nation that our people may be united in good will, understanding, and brotherhood.

Minister and Congregation: Silent prayer

Minister: Guardian of our republic and Keeper of our destiny, let thy Spirit move among our people that they may seek goodness, truth, and righteousness.

Organist: One verse of a hymn with Amen

84

Scripture: I Chr. 29:10-19 (David's Thanksgiving)

Organist (softly) : One verse of "Sweet Hour of Prayer"

Minister: This is the place of prayer. In these moments of guided meditation each person silently offers his own prayer. Let us all pray:

Let us thank God for the daily providence that sustains us and for special benefits that fill our hearts with gladness.

Minister and Congregation: Silent prayer

Minister: We praise thee, O Lord, for the mercies that are new every morning and fresh every evening.

Organist: Amen

Minister: Let us pray for the homes of our people that children may be brought up in the nurture of the Lord, that the aged may find light at eventide, and that families may rejoice in love and peace and righteousness.

Minister and Congregation: Silent prayer

Minister: Grant thy blessing, O Father, upon parents and children that our homes may be centers of stability and that families may be united in duty and affection.

Organist: Amen

Minister: Let us pray for the Christian fellowship, that the servants of God at home and abroad may have wisdom and strength to meet the needs of this generation.

Minister and Congregation: Silent prayer

Minister: O Lord, who hast bound us together in the bundle of life; hasten the day when all mankind shall seek thee and all nations be at peace with thee.

Organist: Amen

Minister: Let us dedicate ourselves afresh to the service of Christ and his Church.

Minister and Congregation: Silent prayer

Minister: Accept our dedication, O Lord, that through us thy kingdom may be served and thy name glorified.

Organist: One verse of a hymn with Amen

85

Scripture: Isa. 40:28-31

Organist (softly) : One verse of "Spirit of God, Descend upon My Heart"

Minister: In these moments of guided meditation each person silently offers his own prayer. Let us pray:

Let us rest quietly upon God and pray that tides of divine power may fill our waiting souls.

Minister and Congregation: Silent prayer

Minister: As we rest in the quietness, O Lord, may we find the perfect peace promised to those whose minds are stayed on thee.

Organist: Amen

Minister: Let us offer our petitions for those who need divine guidance as they make important decisions, that they may choose the right path.

Minister and Congregation: Silent prayer

Minister: O Lord, who art the light and salvation of all who seek thee; we beseech thy favor for those whom we name in our hearts, that they may be strong and of a good courage.

Organist: Amen

Minister: Let us pray for the men and women from this church who have gone to far places as heralds of Christ, that their message may be received as glad tidings of salvation.

Minister and Congregation: Silent prayer

Minister: Grant unto thy servants, O God, a renewal of inner power that they may have joy in their labors and success in their endeavors.

Organist: Amen

Minister: Let us bring to God the secret desires of our hearts and pray that he may answer our petitions according to his wisdom and love.

Minister and Congregation: Silent prayer

Minister: O Father, who art more willing to answer our prayers than we are to offer them; fulfill now the desires of thy servants according to thy goodness and mercy.

We offer all our petitions in the name and spirit of Jesus Christ our Saviour.

Organist: One verse of a hymn with Amen

86

Scripture: Ps. 100

Minister: This is the house of prayer. As we bow before God in quietness, each person offers his own prayer. Let us pray.

Organist: One stanza of "Dear Lord and Father of Mankind"

Minister: Let us offer our gratitude for the comradeship of friends, the laughter of children, the experiences that make us glad, and for all life's goodness.

Minister and Congregation: Silent prayer

Minister: We praise thee, O Lord, for the goodness and mercy that crown our days.

Organist: Amen

Minister: Let us ask God's blessing that our work may be sanctified, our wounds healed, our hopes renewed, and our better selves quickened.

Minister and Congregation: Silent prayer

Minister: Renew in us a right spirit, O Father, that we may rejoice as strong men to run a race.

Organist: Amen

Minister: Let us pray for the sick and discouraged, and for all who have a place in our hearts and sympathies, that they may be strengthened by the comfort of God.

Minister and Congregation: Silent prayer

Minister: Be thou the shining Companion of those to whom we are bound by dear ties of affection. Give them hope and courage and unshakable faith.

Organist: Amen

Minister: Let us pray for our church and its fellowship, that we may worthily worship God and consistently follow Christ.

Minister and Congregation: Silent prayer

Minister: Hear our prayers, O Lord. May the meditations of our hearts be acceptable unto thee. And grant us thy peace.

Organist: One verse of a hymn with Amen

87

Scripture: Phil. 4:4-7 (R.S.V.)

Organist (softly) : One verse of "Breathe on Me, Breath of God"

Minister: The scripture bids us let our requests be made known unto God with thanksgiving. In these moments of meditation each person offers his own silent prayer.

Let us thank God for the beauty of the world, the satisfaction of life's adventure, and the greatness of our Christian heritage. Let us all pray:

Minister and Congregation: Silent prayer

Minister: We praise thee for every satisfying experience. For harvests gathered, victories won, and advances gained, we lift our hearts in gratitude.

Organist: Amen

Minister: Let us pray for the members of this church and for persons who have recently made their confession of Christ as Saviour, that they may have daily strength for daily needs.

Minister and Congregation: Silent prayer

Minister: Bless all members of our fellowship, O Lord, that they may continually rejoice in thy goodness and mercy.

Organist: Amen

Minister: Let us pray for the progress of the kingdom, that God will send laborers into his harvest field.

Minister and Congregation: Silent prayer

Minister: Inspire thy Church, O Lord of the living harvest, that thy people may work for the increasing transformation of the world into thy kingdom.

Organist: Amen

Minister: Let us remember at the throne of grace all who remember us in their prayers and all for whom our prayers are desired, that God will abundantly answer their prayers in wisdom and love.

Minister and Congregation: Silent prayer

Minister: Unto thy gracious keeping, O Father, we commend all who are bound to us by ties of affection, beseeching thee to guide them in all their ways.

These petitions we offer in the name of Jesus Christ our Saviour.

Organist: One verse of a hymn with Amen

88

Scripture: Isa. 35:8-10

Minister: This is the house of God. We assemble in this place of prayer to renew our souls, recapture our visions, and reconsecrate ourselves to Christian obedience and service.

Organist (softly): One verse of "Take Time to Be Holy"

Minister: In these moments of guided meditation we open our minds to the flowing tides of the divine Spirit. Each person silently offers his own petitions. Let us pray:

Let us confess our neglected vows and broken promises, the sins we acknowledge and those we dare not name. And in penitence let us ask God's forgiveness.

Minister and Congregation: Silent prayer

Minister: Help us, O Lord, to see our conduct against the background of Calvary. And in the name of him who was crucified for sin, grant us thy pardon.

Organist: Amen

Minister: Let us offer our gratitude for life's healing ministries: for times of quietness, for refreshing friendship, for renewed hope, and for many springs of joy.

Minister and Congregation: Silent prayer

Minister: Thanks be to thee, O God, who hast woven goodness and mercy into the fabric of all our days.

Organist: Amen

Minister: Let us pray for divine guidance in our daily life that we may choose what is right and good, and be preserved from evil.

Minister and Congregation: Silent prayer

Minister: Direct us, O Lord, along the way we should go. Lighten our path that we may know where we may safely tread. Lead us in the paths of righteousness for thy name's sake.

Organist: Amen

Minister: Let us pray for Christians throughout the world that they may enter into deeper fellowship with God and closer union with one another.

Minister and Congregation: Silent prayer

Minister: Look with favor, O Father, upon thy Church and hasten the day when there shall be one fold and one Shepherd. So may thy kingdom come and thy will be done.

Organist: Amen

Minister: Let us bring to God our secret desires in the confidence that he is the Giver of every good gift.

Minister and Congregation: Silent prayer

Minister: Fulfill the desires of thy servants, O Lord, as thou seest good; through Jesus Christ our Lord.

Organist: One verse of a hymn with Amen

X

The Offering

89

Gracious Father, whose mercies are new every morning and fresh every evening; help us to respond to thy constant goodness with wholehearted fidelity. May we dedicate our gifts of heart and mind and substance to the service of thy kingdom. So govern us by thy Spirit that we may serve the welfare of mankind and the glory of thy name; through Jesus Christ our Lord. AMEN.

90

Thou, O Lord, hast made known the gospel of redemption through human lips and fashioned the fellowship of reconciliation through thy Church. Accept the offerings which now we present as a token of our love for thee and loyalty to thy Church; through Jesus Christ our Saviour. AMEN.

91

O Lord God, who crownest our years with thy goodness and redeemest our lives from destruction; we praise thee for all the gifts of thy providence. Freely we have received. May we freely give, that thy kingdom may come and that thy will may be done in our hearts, in this church, and throughout the world. We make our offering in the name of Jesus Christ our Lord. AMEN.

92

Eternal God, who hast bidden us let our light so shine before men that they may see our good works and glorify thee; grant us grace to render a good account of our stewardship; through Jesus Christ our Lord. AMEN.

93

O God, Author of all goodness, who hast entrusted us with material possessions and made us stewards of thy bounty; accept the offerings which now we render unto thee; through Jesus Christ our Lord. AMEN.

94

Lord of all worlds and lover of all mankind, we dedicate to thee our minds that we may think thy thoughts after thee, our hearts that they may beat in harmony with thy will, and our bodies that they may fulfill thy purpose. And now we offer of our substance that thy kingdom may prosper in this community and be proclaimed to the uttermost parts of the earth; through Jesus Christ our Redeemer. AMEN.

XI

Prayer on Specific Scripture

95

"Finally, . . . be strong in the Lord . . ."
Eph. 6:10-17

Lord God of hosts, who hast called us to serve beneath the banner of the cross; prepare us to fight the good fight as good soldiers of the Lord Jesus.

Strengthen us in our Christian convictions that we may be girded with truth and guarded against error. Fortify us with righteousness that we may never be ashamed to stand up for Jesus. Keep us alert against temptation and make us bold to proclaim the gospel of peace.

Deepen our confidence in thy goodness that

our faith may turn aside the arrows of evil.
Cover our heads with the helmet of salvation
that we may be protected from harm. Stir our
hearts by the inspiration of thy Spirit that in
the day of battle we may stand firm and hold
our ground.

Use us, O God, in the struggle for truth and
righteousness and peace. Increase our faith.
Grant us salvation. And inspire us by thy
word. We offer our prayer in the name of
Jesus Christ our Lord. AMEN.

96

"The Lord is my Shepherd . . ."
Ps. 23

Shepherd of souls, under whose protection
all our days are spent; we lift our hearts to
thee in gratitude. We thank thee for the daily
providence which supplies our material needs.
We praise thee for the joys of friendship, the
love of dear ones, and the affection that satisfies the heart. We rejoice in the quietness of
mind that comes to us through the fellowship

of prayer and in the peace which the world can neither give nor take away.

Lead us in the paths of righteousness. Preserve us from foolish blunders. Sustain us through life's troubles. When our night is dark, let our sky be lighted by stars of hope. When our burdens are heavy, let our strength be equal to our tasks. And when we walk through the valley of the shadows and are touched by pain and awed by mystery, let us fear no evil for thou art with us.

Sanctify to us the blessings we have received as thy guests at the banquet of life. Through all the years thy power has upheld us, thy love has led us, thy grace has refreshed us. Thou hast been our refuge and our strength. Help us to respond to thy goodness and mercy with our heart's devotion. We make our dedication in the name of the Good Shepherd, Jesus Christ our Lord. AMEN.

97

"Our Father which art in heaven . . ."
Matt. 6:9-13

Hallowed be thy name, O Lord, for thy goodness never fails. Age after age the living wait on thee, and thou givest them their meat in due season. Our fathers in their pilgrimage walked by thy guidance and were comforted by thy presence. Still to their children be as the cloud by day and the fire by night. Let us travel the King's highway with rejoicing and arrive at our goal in peace.

Through all the days thy mercy has been with us. Thy providence has sustained us, and thy love has lighted our way. Continue thy mercies, O Lord. Give us day by day our daily bread. And grant that we may welcome each dawn with serene trust and firm faith.

Look upon us with compassion as we confess our shortcomings. We have failed to love thee with our whole heart and strength and mind, and we have failed to love our neighbor as ourselves. May the memory of our failures keep us humble before thee and charitable

107

toward others. Help us to show the love that bears all things, believes all things, hopes all things, and endures all things. Forgive us our offenses and give us grace to forgive those who trespass against us.

Strengthen us in our conflict with temptation. Arm us with the breastplate of righteousness and the sword of the spirit. Deliver us from the power of evil. And to thee shall be all honor and glory, power and dominion, both now and ever. AMEN.

XII

Pastoral Prayer: General

98

Eternal God, who hast refreshed us through the mystery of sleep and awakened us to the adventure of the new day; satisfy us with the assurance of thy presence. May the knowledge of thy nearness make us glad.

Teach us to unseal springs of joy. Open our eyes to the glint of beauty in unexpected places. Stir our minds to catch hints of the eternal in the swiftly passing days. And incline our hearts to look for good in all things.

We thank thee for home and church and country and all the blessings of our Christian heritage. Help us to measure up to our responsibilities. As we have freely received, so may we freely give. As we have been blessed through the love and devotion and toil of others, so may we convey some spiritual service to all who come within the range of our influence.

We praise thee for thy Son, who was wounded for our transgressions and bruised for our iniquities. By his stripes we are healed. Let us never forget the price he paid for our salvation. And grant that in remembering him we may learn something of the height and depth, the length and breadth and everlasting splendor, of thy love.

To thy compassion we commend all who endure trial. Bless those who walk in loneliness or wait in grief, and those burdened with care or thrust aside from the active stream of life. Lighten their pathway. Comfort their hearts. And strengthen them with faith in thy goodness.

Let thy blessing rest upon all servants of thy kingdom. As they serve human welfare through the kingdom of love, joy, and peace, may they have power for witness and success in their service.

Regard with thy favor all who have a place in our hearts and sympathies. Protect them with the Christian's armor that in the day of temptation they may stand firm. Shelter them in times of trouble that in thy pavilion they may find peace. Lift upon them the light of thy countenance that their every joy may be increased.

We commend ourselves to thy gracious keeping. Be thou our inspiration when we leave this sanctuary and take up again the common ways of life. Make us eager to face the adventures that await us on the Christian highroad.

Prosper our ways as thou seest good that we may go forward in thy strength. Increase in us the power of great convictions that our lives may be strong and wholesome. Waken the warrior blood in our sleepy veins that we may endure hardship as good soldiers of Christ Jesus.

Help us, O Lord, to fight evil, promote

goodness, and serve mankind. In all things may we do thy will. And when we kneel before thee at the end of the day, may our shield of faith be without blemish or stain. We offer our prayer in the name of Jesus Christ our Lord. AMEN.

99

Almighty and most merciful Father, whose love has lighted our pathway; grant us thy blessing, we beseech thee, as we offer our praise, make our intercessions, and present our supplications.

We rejoice in this break in the common day when we may turn aside from the clamor of the world and permit divine harmonies to flow into our minds. May our ears never be dull to the divine splendor. Despite the familiarity of the written words and the limitations of the human medium through which they are given, may the message of this hour bring peace and power, healing and inspiration.

We rejoice in our freedom. Inspire us to choose wisely between good and evil, right and wrong, harmony and discord. Forbid that we should fall into bondage to evil thoughts, evil habits, evil deeds. Keep us completely free. And when moments of high inspiration come, may we be able to accept the challenge and march steadily on.

We rejoice in every gracious encouragement we have received or given. Teach us to enthrone wisdom upon our tongues. And grant that we may pass on to others such kindness and understanding as we would they should show unto us.

To thy compassion we commend those who dwell where disappointment crushes or sickness lingers or sorrow broods. May they find comfort through the strength of faith, the light of hope, and the assurance of thy love.

Look with favor upon truehearted young people who seek the glory of the lighted mind. May they hold fast their dreams. Teach them how to redeem the time lest their hopes vanish in the fogs of despair. Strengthen them with

113

the companionship of him who is the light, the truth, and the way.

To thy gracious keeping we commend all our dear ones. Bless the children of our homes, the comrades of daily life, and the friends from whom we are separated by time and distance. Strengthen them in weakness, deliver them in temptation, and preserve them in peril.

When we leave this house of prayer, may the benediction of thy presence continue to illumine our souls, encourage our hearts, and guide our feet. Enlighten our souls that we may be quick to detect the easy wrong and eager to stand firm for the right. May we endure as seeing him who is invisible. Inspire our hearts with courage that we may be courageous in thought, word, and deed. May we put on the Christian armor and be able to withstand the assaults of evil. Guide our feet into paths of service that we may impart some blessing to all whom we meet on life's highway. These our prayers we offer in the name of Jesus Christ our Lord. Amen.

100

O Lord, who hast turned back the curtain of night and caused the light of a new day to touch the earth with beauty; dispel the darkness from our minds, we beseech thee, and renew in us the light of faith and hope and love.

Grant us firmer faith in life's possible splendor and greater eagerness to measure up to life's demands. Teach us to overcome inertia and complacency and make us willing to pay the price of Christian character.

Let our eyes be bright with hope and our hands useful in service. Let our lips be ready to pray and our hearts be filled with kindness.

We praise thee for daily strength for daily need. Thy word is a lamp unto our feet and a light unto our path. Thy love is our shelter in the time of storm. Thy whisper is our strength and courage in the quiet hour. And thy hand is our support as we climb difficult places or trudge along valleys of disappointment.

We remember before thee the boys and

115

girls of our hearts and homes. Satisfy them with all needed good. And grant that the unfolding years may bring them strength of character and beauty of spirit.

Let thy favor rest upon the young men and women. As they mature in knowledge and experience, may they learn to do justly, love mercy, and walk humbly with thee.

We bring to thy mercy seat all who are troubled and anxious and fearful. Refresh them with quietness and confidence. Give them courage to endure. And grant them the sure knowledge that thou art with them through all changes, in darkness and in light, in sorrow and in joy, in adversity and in prosperity.

We offer our petitions in the all-prevailing name of Jesus Christ our Lord. AMEN.

101

Eternal God, who hast created the heavens and the earth and all that dwell therein, and who hast set the divine spirit in man that he may think thy thoughts after thee; we dare to claim thee as our Father, for thou hast made us in thine own image.

We come before thee as children and confess our failures and misdeeds. Thou didst entrust us with good fortune, and we failed to share thy bounty. We withheld our portion from the needy and closed our ears to the cry of the unfortunate.

Thou didst give us a vision of life's splendid possibilities, and we allowed the dream to fade in the light of the common day. We turned aside from the strait gate and narrow way which leads unto life and chose the easy path of least resistance.

Thou didst surround us with friends and dear ones who made sacrifices on our behalf, and we failed in gratitude. We permitted watching eyes to lose their sparkle and waiting hearts to lose hope because we did not care enough.

With humility we confess our selfishness, our indifference, our lack of brotherly love. Thou knowest our frailty. Our secret sins are

117

not hidden from thee. Accept our penitence. Pardon our offenses. And deliver us from our sins that we may walk before thee in newness of life.

We beseech thee, O Father, to release us from all imprisoning yesterdays. Open our eyes to wider horizons. Help us to lay aside every weight and to run with patience the race that is set before us.

Inspire us with the spirit of adventure. Make us willing to blaze new trails, welcome new friendships, seize new opportunities for service. So may we forget the things that are behind and reach forward to the things that are ahead, looking unto Jesus, the pioneer and perfecter of our faith.

We thank thee, O God, for the love that crowns our days. Thy mercies are as the stars for multitude. Great is thy faithfulness. Thou hast set us in a world of beauty and harmony. We rejoice in the loveliness of the dawn and the glory of the evening, in the whisper of the wind among the trees and the fleck of light and shade upon the branches, in the fragrance of flowers and the beauty of the sky.

Thou hast supplied our needs for body, mind, and spirit. We rejoice in daily food and all material benefits, in mental growth through mental struggle, in deepened understanding of the meaning of life, and in the inner voice that tells us we are thine.

Thou hast given us a place in the fellowship of thy Church. We rejoice in Christian friendships and Christian worship, in opportunities for service and in the redeeming love of the Saviour.

For all thy mercies we offer our tribute of gratitude. Help us to respond to thy great goodness by loving thee with all our heart and soul, strength and mind.

We remember before thee, O Lord, all for whom our intercessions are desired, all who have an interest in our prayers, and all whose lives we touch in our daily activities.

Let the beauty of thy peace descend upon those who are fretful and anxious. Help them to be still and know that thou art God. So

119

may they gain strength through quietness and confidence.

Comfort the lonely and troubled. Teach them to bring their burdens to thee in the assurance of thy wisdom and love. So may they learn that thy compassions fail not and that thou art mighty to save.

Reveal thy goodness to the sick in body and mind. Give them patience and courage. Restore them in faith and hope. So may they rejoice in thy renewing power and healing presence.

We surrender ourselves, O Father, to thy gracious keeping. Illumine our minds with divine truth. Satisfy our hearts with thy love. Lead our feet into paths of righteousness. And through all life's adventure grant us serene trust in thy goodness. We offer our prayer in the name of our Saviour Jesus Christ. AMEN.

XIII

Certain Days and Occasions

102
Christmas Eve and Christmas
I

Gracious God, who hast revealed thyself to mankind through the Child of Bethlehem; accept the devotion that now we offer. May the spirit of this Christmas season so possess us that we may worship thee in the beauty of holiness. The dayspring from on high hath visited us and revealed thy glory, and we bow before thee in gratitude. We glorify thee for the divine mystery of Christmas and rejoice in its tidings of redemption. We thank thee for the human tenderness of Christmas and rejoice in its tidings of love. We magnify thy name for the glorious promise of Christmas and rejoice in its tidings of peace on earth and good will to men.

We confess our waywardness and impatience. Our hearts have often been busy inns that had no room for thee. Our ears have been closed to the song of the angels, and our eyes have been dimmed to the splendor of Bethlehem. Forgive our blindness. Quicken our spirits. Make us sensitive to the everlasting presence of him who is the Light of the world.

Unto thy gracious keeping we commend ourselves. The light of the Christmas star illumines our way. Sustain us in days of routine. Guide us in all new adventure. Keep us on the highway of Christian truth. And give us grace to lay before our King the gold of obedience, the incense of lowliness, and the myrrh of healing friendship. We offer our prayer in the name of the Babe of Bethlehem, our Saviour and Lord. AMEN.

122

II

O Lord, our Lord, who hast prepared for them that love thee such joys as surpass man's hopes; hear us as we invoke thy blessing upon those who have a place in our hearts and sympathies. Enlighten the minds of boys and girls and young people that they may find joy in following the Master. Grant thy blessing upon those who rejoice in new-found happiness that they may know the joy of continuing salvation. Let the angel of thy presence inspire those who communicate the spirit of Christmas through their own radiant good will, that they may find gladness and comfort and peace.

We bring to thee those whose lives are shadowed by care and anxiety, praying that they may be comforted. May the Sun of Righteousness arise for them with healing in his wings. Satisfy the restless ones who search for peace. May the light of the Christmas star lead them to him who is the answer to their prayers, the satisfaction of their longings, and their heart's true home. Lead them by thy love; support them by thy strength;

gladden them by thy presence. So may they enter into the joy of this gracious season by enthroning Jesus Christ as their King, to whom with thee and the Holy Spirit be glory forever and ever. AMEN.

103

The New Year

I

Blessed and eternal God, by whose mercies we are come to the dawn of another year; prepare us in heart and mind for the continuing journey that we may press on to the prize of our high calling in Christ Jesus.

Set us free from all imprisoning yesterdays. Let us break loose from the fetters that bind us to an ignoble past. Make us strong to overcome the enchantment of evil. May we see our lives against the background of Calvary and our sins in the light of the love of him who hung and suffered there. And grant that we may be so penitent for the wrongs we have

124

done, so honest in the effort to make amends, and so resolute in our eagerness to do the right that we may be delivered by thy pardon from the haunting memory of our transgressions. We offer our prayer in the name of him who makes all things new, even Jesus Christ our Lord. AMEN.

II

Blessed art thou, O Lord, who hast brought us in peace to the beginning of this new year. We cross into its frontiers with gratitude at the remembrance of thy goodness and mercy. We thank thee for the beauty of the earth, the satisfactions of friendship, and all simple things that unseal springs of joy. We praise thee for aspirations that have been fulfilled. Hopes that seemed too good to be true have been realized. Duties that were drudgery have been transfigured by the kindling touch of love. And burdens that troubled the spirit have become sources of strength.

Quicken in us the awareness that thy good-

125

ness never fails and that thy mercy endures forever. Let us go forward with strength and rejoicing for thou art our unseen Companion. And through all the changing scenes of life, amid the shadows of time and the ebb and flow of our days, may we become more like him whom to know is life eternal. And to thee shall be all power and glory both now and ever. AMEN.

104

Easter

I

Blessed and eternal God, who hast given unto us the power of an endless life and hast opened to us a new and living way through the resurrection of thy Son Jesus Christ; look favorably upon us this day that we may rejoice in a great salvation.

We thank thee for the resurrection joy which overcomes darkness and despair and touches common days with light and gladness. We praise thee for the resurrection power

126

which breaks the reign of sin and death and imparts courage and high resolve and new life. We glorify thee for the resurrection victory which transforms bitterness into thanksgiving, tragedy into triumph, and sorrow into quiet peace. Grant unto us a larger measure of the joy and power and victory of Easter that we may be effective witnesses for our Master. We ask in his name. AMEN.

II

Eternal God, unfailing source of mercy and power, who hast taught us by thy blessed Son that we ought always to pray and not to lose heart; hear us as we pray for our kindred and all who are related to us through ties of friendship and sympathy.

Have compassion upon those whose lives are shadowed by fear or anxiety, trouble or grief, that they may be strengthened by the eternal gospel and comforted by the risen Lord. Look with favor upon those who are beset by temptation, that they may be saved from falling by the same power which recalled the disciples to their risen Master in faith and love and fidelity. Give wisdom and strength to ministers and missionaries and all heralds of the risen Christ, that they may fulfill their mission with confidence. Grant thy blessing upon all the races of mankind, that the time may be hastened when all peoples and all nations shall acknowledge Jesus Christ as King of kings and Lord of lords. So may thy Church increase and thy name be glorified.

To thy gracious keeping we commend ourselves. Keep us ever true to the everlasting gospel. Grant that though our outward man perish, the inward man shall be renewed day by day. And bestow upon us the peace that passeth all understanding; through Christ our Redeemer. AMEN.

105

Children's Day

I

Father everlasting, for whom every family in heaven and on earth is named; we thank thee for the joyous memories of this anniversary. Grant that on this day of gladness we may learn to love thee more and serve thee better.

We pray for thy blessing upon parents, teachers, guardians, and all who are entrusted with the welfare of boys and girls. May they live as wise and worthy examples. Let them be as a shelter and strength and guiding light. Give them skill to win the love and trust of the children. So may they receive responsive affection from the young lives committed to their care. We offer our prayer in the name of him who set a little child in the midst and said, "Of such is the kingdom of heaven." AMEN.

II

Dear Lord and Father of mankind, who didst entrust thy well-beloved Son to the love and discipline of a humble home; we beseech thy blessing upon children everywhere. Let the arms of thy compassion comfort those who are lonely or neglected, that they may know

129

they are precious in thy sight. Raise up
champions for victims of oppression, that
good will may triumph and justice be served.
Regard with thy gracious favor the children
of our hearts and homes. As they grow in body
and mind, may they develop also in spirit.
Give them grace to grow in the knowledge of
thee, the love of thy Church, and the joy of
serving Christ. Bless the children from whom
we are separated by time or distance. Guard
them from peril and evil. Give them the sure
confidence that thou art always their refuge
and strength. And grant that neither time nor
distance may break the bonds of love that
bind us to one another and to thee. We offer
our petitions in the name of him who took
little children in his arms and blessed them,
even Jesus Christ our Saviour. AMEN.

106

National Anniversary

I

God of our land and Keeper of our destiny,
we beseech thy blessing upon our country.

May the fresh wind of thy power blow through all areas of our national life. Direct the hearts of home builders, that the homes of our nation may be centers of understanding, harmony, and stability. Direct the efforts of social workers, that dwellers in congested cities may have brighter prospects for life, liberty, and the pursuit of happiness. Direct the policies of educators, that the schools of our land may be centers of sound learning, wise discipline, and good character, and that boys and girls may be trained in ways of righteousness. Direct the minds of lawmakers, that this nation may have a new birth of freedom—freedom from fear, freedom from prejudice, freedom to grow in brotherhood. Deepen our understanding of the righteousness that exalteth a nation. Teach us the arts of peace and service. So incline our people to do thy will that our nation may be a blessing to all mankind. We offer our prayer in the name of him who taught human brotherhood and died for all men's salvation, even Jesus Christ our Lord. AMEN.

131

II

God of the nations, by whose providence we are citizens of a land of hope and glory; we rejoice in our heritage of faith and freedom.

We praise thee for pilgrims who crossed perilous seas, carved homes out of the wilderness, and established a community on foundations of righteousness. We praise thee for leaders who in times of crisis pledged to one another their lives, their fortunes, and their honor, that liberty might be preserved.

We thank thee for heroes tested in the fires of war. They heard the call and kept faith with the patriot dream. They turned from home and dear ones. And in distant places they fought in liberating strife that government of the people, by the people, for the people, might not perish from the earth.

We thank thee for scientists and inventors, ministers and educators, and all those whose physical toil, mental ability, and spiritual consecration built up this nation in strength and righteousness.

For the joy we have found through citizenship in this land of freedom and for the many benefits that have come to us through the fidelity of men and women who kept faith with their ideals, we thank thee. Help us to prove our gratitude by serving our generation and passing on the torch to those who will come after us.

Grant thy blessing upon the President of the United States, his advisers, and members of Congress. Give wisdom and the strength of righteous convictions to governors of the states and all others entrusted with the welfare of the people. May they wisely use their authority to advance the common good.

We offer our prayer and our dedication in the name of Jesus, our Saviour and Lord. AMEN.

107

Thanksgiving Day
I

O God, Author of all goodness, truth, and beauty; we rejoice in all thy mercies and lift our hearts and voices in gratitude.

Thou hast given us to play our part in a world of beauty and wonder. We rejoice in the changing seasons: the quickening energy of spring, the growing power of summer, the ripening process of autumn, and the white restfulness of winter. We thank thee for the beauty of the earth and the splendor of the skies, for majestic mountains and picturesque valleys, for running streams and rolling prairies, for trees, shrubs, flowers, and all loveliness of nature.

We thank thee for companionships on the journey of life. For love's fidelity and friendship's service, we praise thee. Make us worthy of our friends that watching eyes may not grow dim nor waiting hearts grow cold through our neglect.

We rejoice in the heritage into which we are come. Others have labored, and we have entered into their labors. Laws, freedom, truth, and righteousness came with the exiles across the waves. Help us to be worthy of our heritage in the land of the free and the home of the brave. And grant that we may leave behind us some contribution to the enrichment of mankind. Receive, O Father, this prayer of joyous gratitude offered in the name of Jesus Christ our Lord. AMEN.

II

We praise thee, O God, for thou art gracious. We rejoice in thee, O Lord, for thou art our salvation. We give thanks to thee, O Father, for thou art the Giver of every good and perfect gift. With grateful hearts we offer our tribute of thanksgiving.

We thank thee for the adventure of life. Thou hast given to us a span of time that we may fill with worthy purpose and joyous adventure. Each morning we may rejoice in the day thou hast made and be glad in it. May we so conduct ourselves through the waking hours that when evening comes the ship of our life may bear cargoes of fragrant memories and joyous achievement.

We praise thee for the daily mercies by which our lives are sustained. Keep us ever mindful of thy providence, for we cannot draw a single breath or grow a single grain of wheat apart from thee. Thou openest thy hand and satisfiest the desire of every living thing.

We glorify thee for thy plan of salvation and for him who revealed thee to us. May our lives show forth the gratitude of our hearts for thy most wondrous gift.

Accept our praise and thanksgiving, offered in the name of Jesus Christ, our Redeemer. Amen.

XIV

Litanies and Responsive Prayers

108
Litany of Praise

Almighty and everlasting God, who hast set eternity in man's heart so that he finds fulfillment only in thee; accept our heart's devotion and grant that we may worship thee in the beauty of holiness.

We praise thee, Holy Father, for our creation, preservation, and all the blessings of this mortal life:

We praise thee, eternal Father.

We praise thee, Holy Saviour, for thy victory over death and for the kingdom of heaven thou dost open to those who put their trust in thee:

We praise thee, eternal Saviour.

We praise thee, Holy Spirit, for the light and truth and comfort thou dost impart to all believers:

We praise thee, eternal Spirit.

O Lord, our Creator, our Redeemer, our ever-present Companion, hear these our prayers, grant that our conduct may be well-pleasing in thy sight, and let our lives magnify thy holy name.

Amen.

109

Litany of Thanksgiving

Father of all mercies and God of all comfort, whose bountiful care provides for all our needs of body, mind, and spirit; we offer thee our tribute of gratitude.

For the new life of spring, the growth of summer, the harvest of autumn, the restfulness of winter, and all the wonder of the changing seasons:

138

We praise thee, O God, and bless thy name.

For daily food which sustains the physical frame and the bread of life which feeds the soul:

We praise thee, O God, and bless thy name.

For friendship's fidelity and love's understanding and all satisfying companionships:

We praise thee, O God, and bless thy name.

For laws and freedom, truth and righteousness, and all the benefits of our national heritage:

We praise thee, O God, and bless thy name.

For the adventure of life with its light and laughter, joys and friendship, labor and achievement:

We praise thee, O God, and bless thy name.

For the evidence of thy love revealed in Jesus Christ our Lord, the comfort and joy of the Scriptures, and all the blessings that come to us through the Christian faith:

We praise thee, O God, and bless thy name.
Amen.

110

Morning Litany

O Lord, our Strength and our Redeemer, who hast brought us to the beginning of this new day in peace; grant that all our doings, begun, continued, and fulfilled in thee, may be righteous in thy sight.

Shape us to thy purpose as clay is fashioned by the potter, that we may be worthy servants of thy kingdom:

Use us, O Lord.

Guide us in the hour of decision, that we may be saved from error and led into paths of righteousness:

Lead us, O Lord.

Help us to learn obedience to the heavenly vision that we may travel the Christian highway with confidence and joy:

Teach us, O Lord.

Defend us in the time of temptation, deliver us in the hour of danger, and grant us the victory for thy name's sake:

Preserve us, O Lord.

Use us, lead us, teach us, and preserve us;
through Jesus Christ our Lord.

Amen.

111
Evening Litany

He that dwelleth in the secret place of the
Most High shall abide under the shadow of
the Almighty.

Let our prayer be set forth before thee, O
Lord, as incense, and the lifting up of our
hands as the evening sacrifice:

Hear our prayer, O Lord, and grant us thy
peace.

For friendship's fidelity and love's understanding:

We praise thee, O God.

For work we have been permitted to do, and
the satisfactions we have found in our labors:

We praise thee, O God.

For victory over temptation and the fulfillment of high hopes:

We praise thee, O God.

For the goodness and mercy which have

141

been our companions through all this day:

We praise thee, O God.

Gracious Father, who desireth not the death of a sinner but rather that he may turn from his wickedness and live; be merciful to us as we confess our transgressions:

Be merciful to us, O God.

For all that we have done amiss, or spoken falsely, or purposed against thy will:

Forgive us, O Lord.

For ignorant and hasty faults, and willful and deliberate offenses:

Forgive us, O Lord.

For reluctance to accept responsibility, and all our sins of slothfulness and neglect:

Forgive us, O Lord.

For setting our minds on things seen and temporal and losing sight of things unseen and eternal:

Forgive us, O Lord.

O God our Father, we commend ourselves and our dear ones to thy gracious mercy and protection.

That thou wilt take us into thy holy keep-

ing and grant us peace and quietness during
the coming night:

We beseech thee, O Father.

That thou wilt bless our going out and our
coming in from this time forth:

We beseech thee, O Father.

Now unto him that is able to keep us from
falling, and to present us faultless before the
presence of his glory with exceeding joy, to
the only wise God our Saviour, be glory and
majesty, dominion and power, both now and
evermore.

Amen.

112

Litany for Youth

Thou hast made us for thyself, O God, and
our hearts are restless until they rest in thee.
Help us so to seek that we may find, so to
ask that we may receive, so to knock that the
door of new life may be opened unto us.

We acknowledge our failures, O Lord, and
commend ourselves to thy gracious mercy.

For the times when we disobeyed thy commandments and followed our own selfish purposes:

Forgive us, O Lord.

For the times when we were unkind and caused others to suffer:

Forgive us, O Lord.

For the times when we were false to our own ideals and ashamed of our conduct:

Forgive us, O Lord.

Spirit of the living God, who art thyself the great reward of every seeking soul; we praise thee for those things that lead us to a larger life. By the revelation of thyself in Jesus and the message he taught and the life he bestowed:

Teach us and draw us nearer to thyself.

By the joys of friendship, the loyalty of comrades, and the affection of dear ones:

Teach us and draw us nearer to thyself.

By the beauty of the earth, the wonder of the skies, and all of nature's loveliness:

Teach us and draw us nearer to thyself.

By the harvests of field and orchard and

144

sea and all the providence which sustains our lives:

Teach us and draw us nearer to thyself.

By the awareness of man's inhumanity to man, by suffering, frustration, and heartbreak:

Teach us and draw us nearer to thyself.

By the Holy Bible, which is a lamp unto our feet and a light unto our path:

Teach us and draw us nearer to thyself.

Lord of all power and might, sure Guide and Strength of those who put their trust in thee; strengthen us to do thy will and lead us in the way of salvation.

That thy will may be done on earth as i' is in heaven:

We surrender our hearts.

That we may follow the Christ of the Upward Way:

We dedicate our youth.

That we may be channels of blessing to those who come within the range of our influence:

We consecrate our minds.

That we may perform good works with

gladness and fidelity, and do justly, love mercy, and walk humbly with thee:

We present ourselves to thee in grateful devotion.

Now unto him who is able to do exceeding abundantly above all that we ask or think, according to the power that worketh in us, unto him be glory in the Church by Christ Jesus throughout all ages, world without end.

Amen.

113

Responsive Prayer for Men

God so loved the world, that he gave his only begotten Son, that whosoever believeth in him should not perish, but have everlasting life.

Thou, O Lord, who didst call Matthew from the seat of custom and fishermen from their boats and nets:

Grant us grace to accept thee as our Saviour and to follow thee as our Master.

Thou, O Lord, who didst welcome the apostle Peter's confession of faith:

146

Grant that we may enter into a saving knowledge of thee as the eternal Christ and our Saviour.

Thou, O Lord, who didst welcome the inquiry of the Greeks, the faith of the Roman centurion, and the thanks of the grateful Samaritan:

Grant us grace to rise above prejudice for those of different race or creed that our personal relationships may be in harmony with thy love for all mankind.

Thou, O Lord, who didst welcome the support of the disciples who stood by thee in thy trials:

Grand us wisdom to make right decisions at the parting of the ways and courage to pursue the right as thou givest us to see the right.

Thou, O Lord, who didst command thine apostles James and John to fling away ambition and become as little children:

Deliver us from unseemly ambition and grant us the grace of humility.

Thou, O Lord, who didst declare thyself

147

to the apostle Thomas as the Way, the Truth,
and the Life:

*Lead us along the path that we should go
and bring us to our Father's house in peace.*

Thou, O Lord, who didst send forth the
seventy disciples through the cities and vil-
lages of Galilee to prepare for thy coming:

*Use us as ambassadors of good tidings to
all whom we meet on life's highway.*

Thou, O Lord, who wilt judge men at the
last according to their service to the sick and
imprisoned, the poor, hungry, and dispossessed:

*Give us grace to serve the needy in thy
name, to spend and be spent in the ministry
of compassion.*

Now unto him who is able to do exceeding
abundantly above all that we ask or think, according to the power that worketh in us, unto
him be glory in the Church by Christ Jesus
throughout all ages, world without end.

Amen.

114

Responsive Prayer for Women

The hour cometh, and now is, when the true worshipers shall worship the Father in spirit and in truth: for the Father seeketh such to worship him.

Thou, O Lord, who didst open the mind of the woman of Samaria to the nature of the Father:

Grant us some new revealing of truth that shall be a lamp unto our feet and a light unto our path.

Thou, O Lord, who didst speak the word of forgiveness to Mary Magdalene:

Grant us some new understanding of the divine compassion for frail humanity.

Thou, O Lord, who didst welcome the offerings of Mary Magdalene, Joanna, and Susanna for the support of thy disciples:

Grant us wisdom in our giving that we may meet the needs of thy servants in our generation.

Thou, O Lord, who didst honor the love of the Syrophenician mother:

149

Grant us thy blessing in all our family relationships.

Thou, O Lord, who didst lead Martha and Mary into fuller knowledge of the truth:

Grant us grace to make a new consecration of ourselves to the work of thy kingdom.

Thou, O Lord, who didst awaken joy in the hearts of the women who came to the tomb and send them to tell others of thy victory:

Put a new song into our mouths that with lips and lives we may declare the greatness of thy glory.

Now unto the King eternal, immortal, invisible, the only wise God, be honor and glory forever and ever.

Amen.

115

Litany of Praise for the Nation

God of the nations, by whose providence our lives are cast in the pleasant places of this

150

fair land; we bow before thee in gratitude for our heritage of faith and freedom.

For pilgrims who crossed perilous seas, carved homes out of the wilderness, and established communities in righteousness:

We praise thee.

For leaders who pledged to one another their lives, their fortunes, and their sacred honor that liberty might be preserved:

We praise thee.

For heroes tested in the fires of war, who heard the call and kept faith with the patriot dream:

We praise thee.

For statesmen who wrought with patience that government of the people, by the people, for the people, might not perish from the earth:

We praise thee.

For the President of the United States and his advisers, for members of Congress, governors of the states, lawgivers, judges, and all

151

who wisely use their authority to advance the common good:

We praise thee.

For scientists and inventors, ministers and educators, and all whose physical toil, mental ability, and spiritual consecration built up this nation in strength and righteousness:

We praise thee.

For the joy we have known through citizenship in this land of freedom, and for the many benefits that have come to us through the fidelity of men and women who kept faith with their ideals:

We praise thee.

116

Litany for Christmas Eve

Shepherd of the wandering star, who hast revealed thyself to mankind through the Child of Bethlehem; we beseech thee to lead us to the inner meaning of this gracious season that we may worship thee in the beauty of holiness.

For sky-born music to the glory of thy name,

for light to lighten the Gentiles, for revival of hope in a sin-darkened world:

We rejoice and praise thy name.

For the divine wonder of Christmas and its tidings of redemption, for the human tenderness of Christmas and its tidings of love, for the promise of peace on earth to men of good will:

We rejoice and praise thy name.

For the mystery of the Word made flesh, for the light of the knowledge of thy glory revealed in the face of Christ Jesus, for the commission of thine only begotten Son to be the Saviour of mankind:

We rejoice and praise thy name.

That our minds be not closed to the wondrous story of redemption, but that we may be alert to the signs of thy coming:

Hear us, O Christ.

That our wills be not unstable but that we may be resolute to go forward in faith, hope, and love:

Hear us, O Christ.

That our hearts be not as crowded inns but that we may receive thee:

Hear us, O Christ.

Hear us, O Christ, that we may have grace to offer thee the fine gold of obedience, the fragrant incense of humility, and the healing myrrh of our heart's devotion:

Amen.

XV

After the Sermon

117

Servants of the Church

O Lord God, who hast caused many and rich blessings to flow into our lives through thy Church; help us to serve her well. Grant that through our fidelity the influence of the Church may increase and her helpfulness to mankind be extended; through Jesus Christ our Lord. AMEN.

118

Deeper Dedication

Lead us this day, O Father, into deeper dedication to things unseen and eternal. May we carry on our daily activities as those who rejoice in a great salvation. Grant that in thought, speech, and conduct we may glorify thy name. We ask in the spirit of Christ our Redeemer. AMEN.

119

Serene and Confident

Gracious Father, in whom is the fullness of light and love and power; accept our gratitude for all thy mercies. And grant that when we leave this place of worship and walk again in the common ways of everyday, we may be so illumined by thy light, so moved by thy love, and so strengthened by thy power that we shall be serene and confident; through Jesus Christ our Lord. AMEN.

120

The Light upon Our Way

Eternal God, in whom is no darkness at all; we commend ourselves to thy gracious keeping. Thou art our hope and strength and guide. Shed light upon our pathway that we may know where we may safely tread. And when the shadows lengthen and our work is done, bring us to our goal in peace; through Jesus Christ our Lord. AMEN.

121

Christian Friendships

We rejoice, O Father, in the adventure of Christian friendships. Help us to look outward and see others as souls for whom Christ died; help us to look inward and see ourselves as instruments of thy purpose of redemption; help us to look upward and know thee whom to know is life eternal. We offer our petition in the name of Jesus, the great Friend of all mankind. AMEN.

122

In God's Image

O Lord our God, who hast made man in thine own image and given him power to love

157

thee and to think thy thoughts after thee; so work in our hearts that we may perfectly love thee and worthily magnify thy holy name. Amen.

123

Fragile Vessels of Clay

O God, who hast given us the treasure of life in frail vessels of clay, that we may know that all power comes from thee; grant us grace to find beauty and strength and satisfaction in him who brought the more abundant life, even Jesus Christ our Lord. Amen.

124

Shepherd of Souls

Shepherd of our souls, whose presence has been with us through all the days of our pilgrimage; we praise thee for all thy mercies. Help us to respond to thy great goodness with glad devotion; through Jesus Christ our Lord. Amen.

158

125

The Constant Presence

O Lord, in whom we live and move and have our being, and through whom we find rest for our souls; grant unto us a deeper awareness of thy constant presence. May the knowledge of thy nearness fill us with a sense of joyous power. And let us return to life's common ways with high resolve to be more worthy of our heritage as thy children; through Jesus Christ our Lord. AMEN.

126

Horizons of Faith

Enlarge our horizons, O Lord, that we may see our spiritual possibilities. Help us to commit ourselves to thee in full and glad surrender. And lead us in the paths of righteousness for thy name's sake. AMEN.

Index

Figures refer to prayer numbers. CAPITALS *denote titles.*

INDEX

Figures refer to prayer numbers. CAPITALS *denote titles.*

Figures refer to prayer numbers. CAPITALS *denote titles.*

INDEX

Figures refer to prayer numbers. CAPITALS *denote titles.*

163

Figures refer to prayer numbers. CAPITALS *denote titles.*

INDEX

Figures refer to prayer numbers. CAPITALS *denote titles.*

Figures refer to prayer numbers. CAPITALS *denote titles.*

166

INDEX

Figures refer to prayer numbers. CAPITALS *denote titles.*

Figures refer to prayer numbers. CAPITALS *denote titles.*

INDEX

Figures refer to prayer numbers. CAPITALS *denote titles.*

INDEX

Figures refer to prayer numbers. CAPITALS *denote titles.*

Figures refer to prayer numbers. CAPITALS *denote titles.*

INDEX

Figures refer to prayer numbers. CAPITALS *denote titles.*

Figures refer to prayer numbers. CAPITALS *denote titles.*

INDEX

Figures refer to prayer numbers. CAPITALS *denote titles.*

PRAYERS FOR CHRISTIAN SERVICE

Figures refer to prayer numbers. CAPITALS *denote titles.*